the wall is blue

A song of the inner child

LINDA RUTH BROOKS

Chapter quotes and afterword by Dr Steele Fitchett

Copyright © Linda Ruth Brooks 2014
© Steele Fitchett

Cover & interior design © Linda Ruth Brooks

All rights reserved. This book is copyright protected. Apart from any fair dealings for the purpose of private study, criticism, research or review as permitted under the *Copyright Act (Australia)*, no part may be reproduced by any process without written permission. Enquiries should be addressed to the publisher.

ISBN- 978-0-6481902-1-9

Category: family & relationships/spiritual healing

This book, and others by Linda Brooks, may be purchased through amazon.com & online bookstores.

The Wall is Blue is a work of fiction. Any similarity between the characters in this book and real people, living or dead, is coincidental.

Entreat me not to leave you, or to return from following after you: for where you go, I will go; and where you lodge, I will lodge: your people shall be my people, and your God my God:

Ruth 1:16 King James Bible

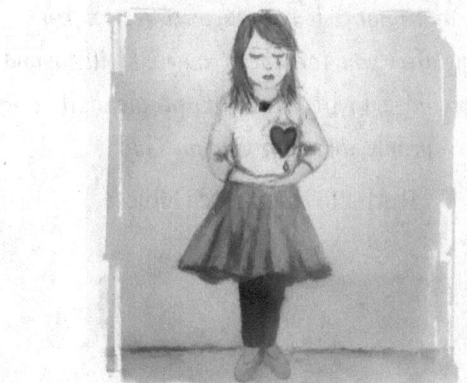

I

One

> *'There is a knowing that comes from a place deeper than thoughts and feelings. It's a knowing that arises in our spirit.'*

Kate couldn't have told anyone when the habit began. It stretched back into a childhood that should still exist, but didn't. It was a habit, pure and simple. Its beginning was unimportant.

There was no clear moment to pin a memory; not like the first time her mother had waved her aside with a moan.

'Are you all right Mummy?'

Mother had turned over with a defeated shrug, burying deeper into a cocoon of dark silence.

'Feed the children.'

As if they were Kate's children and not her's. They were not Emily, Daniel and Sara anymore. And when father turned his key in the front door—*that* would be hers too.

'See to your father, Kate. There's a good girl.'

Kate had never questioned. She met her father with a smile, asked about his day and busied in the kitchen. That's what mother used to do.

At first Kate had stumbled around dropping things and fighting a tight little knot in her stomach. Toasted sandwiches was easy. Then she had learned to use the stovetop.

Father kissed her forehead.

'Where's your mother?'

'Not well today.' Said carefully and neutrally, as if pretending things were normal would make them so. Transform life into a manageable thing. As if ten year olds everywhere were the ladies of the house, the caretakers of the family.

'I see.'

Father didn't change the rhythm, so that helped make it normal. Though deep inside a much younger Kate screamed that it was not. But Emily, Daniel and Sara's voices were louder. Some inner sense stopped Kate from calling them "the children" when speaking to them as was her mother's custom.

She was even particular that she called them in order of their age, oldest to youngest, as if by this precision she could push back the chaos that hovered like a patient bird of prey.

The only evidence of Kate's ambiguity was in the manner she addressed her mother. When she thought of her, she called her Mother, but out loud she called her Mummy. Kate was unaware of this, of course. Children find different voices and Kate was no exception. Perhaps she wanted her mother to be "Mummy" like the mothers she saw at the corner store, or the ones on television. They were Kate's point of reference.

The differences couldn't be avoided then, in those places—the differences in their house, their family. At the supermarket the mothers supervised tots with strident, begging voices and errant feet.

They didn't walk with hurried step and downcast eyes, feeling shame. Shame for her family, the differences, but mainly for herself. She was ashamed of being Kate, the mother. But she could not share confidences leaning over trolleys, or wave cheery greetings.

Presenting crumpled notes at the store and thrusting the change back into her school uniform pocket, Kate had no thought but to get back to Emily, Daniel and Sara.

To make sure they were safe. Back to the house. For that's what it was to her. She had surprised a boy on the school bus when he had tried to make conversation.

'Are you going home?'

He had a kind face.

'I live in a house. It's 23...'

She'd nibbled on her lip, and stopped. It wasn't safe to tell strangers where, or when. Everyone was a stranger. She hadn't made the same mistake again. A boy's baseball cap and a gaze fixed on a book had forestalled the most inquisitive of her travel companions. Those who went to the same school.

Emily sat quietly beside Kate, sheltered in the window seat by her older sister. While other children chatted, whispered and laughed, Kate wondered if she would get home before Daniel and Sara. Hoping the bus wouldn't be delayed.

It was important to be there at the door when Mrs Blakehurst, their babysitter from across the road brought the younger two. It was important to use her grown up voice, through a narrow slit in the door.

'Thank you, Mrs Blakehurst. Here is your pay.'

Passing a stained envelope with cash. Hoping to evade Mrs Blakehurst's questions.

'How is your mother today?'

'She's in the kitchen. She asked me to give you this.'

Mrs Blakehurst's brow furrowed. She opened her mouth to speak.

'The money's all there, Mrs Blakehurst. Ah ... um ... Mother checked it twice.'

Mrs Blakehurst touched Kate's arm.

'You ... I mean ... your mother doesn't have to pay me every day. Once a week would be all right.'

Kate stepped back.

'It's better this way, my ... father ... prefers it.'

Kate bit her tongue and began to close the door, a

stark smile on her face. Daniel's school bag was in the way.

'Shift your bag, Daniel. How many times do I have to remind you?'

Daniel fetched the bag. A little too quickly. His eager face showed panic.

'Thank you, sweetie, please try and remember. For me ... Mother.'

Kate patted his unruly curls, her eyes filled with tenderness.

A strange look flashed over Mrs Blakehurst's round face.

Kate prayed her words and tone were convincing, unaware this was precisely what worried the woman in front of her. Surely Mrs Blakehurst wouldn't suspect that it was Kate, and not her mother, or father who counted out the notes, folding them neatly and placing them in the envelope, then sealing it.

So many lies.

Kate bestowed a wide smile, then closed the door on the outside world. It would be easier now. This, at least was true.

Mother was asleep, or nearly so, in the daybed in the front room. Tiptoeing, Kate moved to the kitchen at the side of the house where three small faces watched her for cues.

'Emily, don't forget to change your uniform. Make

sure Daniel and Sara stay around the back. I'll call you when dinner's ready. It won't be long.'

The earlier dinner was on the table, the easier things would be. Dad had stopped asking who prepared meals.

Two

The first grief in our lives is the failure of our head to connect with our heart.

The kitchen was in the corner of the house. Its large square windows faced the yard on two sides, giving a view of the narrow side walkway as well as the backyard. Kate pulled the kitchen curtains back.

Emily was skipping, her forehead wrinkled with concentration as she counted. 'Twen-*ty* six, twen-*ty* sev-*en*.' Two year old Sara cradled her doll, her fine blonde hair fluttering in baby wisps as she sat on the step down from Daniel. Without appearing to notice her brother, Sara was, as always, never far from him. Daniel, four, paid her no attention as he whispered to Bob, his imaginary friend.

Kate loved this time of day. Tea was a simple repetitive affair, the same veggies and meat every night, making preparation seamless. Cheaper too.

Magenta cherry trees lined the north side of the house

with their waxy shine and dense growth. The high fence at the back would allow slanted rays of afternoon sun for a while yet. Bright crimson fruit buds nestled in the forest green leaves. Soon the trees would be covered with the cream-fluff glory of the flowers, and the ground would be carpeted with their fallen beauty.

Kate slid open the windows, far enough to welcome the southerly breeze, but not past the torn section of the fly screen. There hadn't been enough money for insect repellent this week. Daniel and Sara developed large wheals from mosquito bites, so Kate taped the slash in the screen with masking tape.

Through the lush growth of the magentas Kate could see old Mrs Wentworth filling the bird feeder while she cooed to the birds. The birds warbled their pleasure. Kate sighed. It must be wonderful to be a bird. To have someone whose daily routine provided, and cared.

Kate sighed. It was a shame they couldn't have a puppy for Daniel. Perhaps he wouldn't need an imaginary friend then. But Mother wouldn't cope.

'I can't take care of anything else. The children are enough. A mother can only do so much.'

With a natural rhythm Kate peeled the vegetables as the double boiler built up steam. She'd seen that on television. Some cooking show. Steaming kept the nourishment in the vegetables, or something like that. Anyway, it was important.

'Kate!' Mother's voice. Not low and apologetic, not fragmented or worn. Angry.

Kate swung around to face her mother, knocking the steamer saucepan to the floor. Steam escaped and scalded her arm. She clutched at her forearm with a tea towel. It was a useless gesture. She knew even as she did it, but Mother had that effect.

'Put some butter on it.' Mother was dishevelled, upset.

'Butter doesn't ... it isn't...' Kate reached for the freezer.

Mother sighed when Kate opened the door and took out a packet of frozen peas.

'I hope you're not going to waste those peas, Kaitlin Jane. They aren't cheap. You don't know the meaning of money. You're just a child.'

Kate winced. She applied the frozen packet to the reddened part of her arm.

'They'll still be good for dinner, Mummy.'

Mother snatched the saucepan from the floor.

'I'll get dinner. You don't know what you're doing.'

'But ... nothing's spoiled. It was just the top saucepan— I haven't put the vegetables in yet.'

Kate reached to take the saucepan.

Mother's eyes were fire.

'I don't know what this double cooking pot nonsense is. Where did you learn that? School? We're wasting good money on your education.'

Mother pushed her away from the sink and began scraping the remaining potatoes.

'But it's a public school, Mummy. They don't...'

Kate stared at the floor, counting the chipped Harlequin tiles.

'Oh yes, Kaitlin Jane, I know how much you love school. But you're wasting your time. You'll be lucky to be a wife, and a housekeeper. That's our destiny. It's all women can hope for. You'll understand when you grow up.'

Emily's giggle penetrated the afternoon.

'What have you let the children do?'

Kate straightened, protective.

'Emily, Daniel and Sara are playing in the back yard. Emily changed her uniform and...'

'Quite the little boss, aren't we.'

Mother cut the potatoes roughly.

Kate resisted the urge to point out an area that was still covered in dark skin.

Mother looked at her with careful eyes.

'Daniel's quiet. I suppose he's playing with that fantasy friend of his. There's something wrong with that boy. Takes after his father. A dreamer.'

Kate's muscles clenched.

'He's just...'

Mother spun around.

'What? What is he?'

Mother's eyes flashed. The knife was poised over the pan. She threw the top saucepan in the sink.

'You just made more work. Go and play with the children. But give me those peas.'

Kate handed the bag and blanched at the pain in her arm. She went outside, but she did not play.

She tugged her dress under her to protect her legs from the splintered steps. She wondered if Mrs Blakehurst had balm for burns. It was no use thinking about that. Mother would never allow her to go and ask their babysitter for anything. Kate couldn't remember Mrs Blakehurst ever coming in their house. No, Mother wouldn't let her go. She didn't like interfering people.

~~~

'Is dinner ready? Bob's hungry.'

Kate patted Daniel's head as he sorted his Lego cars. He was too little to understand. A taut pang of protectiveness caught at Kate's heart.

'Mummy's getting dinner tonight.'

The truth. There were enough lies inside their walls. Kate imagined them whirling around like lost pieces of wind and cloud, like a bird seeking to be free, but confused by the transparency of glass.

'Oh, dinner's never as good when she makes it. Bob prob'ly won't eat much.'

Kate smiled at her younger brother, willing it to dispel

the frown on his forehead, but Daniel was not so easily persuaded.

'Why can't you be our mother, Kate?'

Kate had no answer.

A crash from the kitchen muddied her thoughts.

Followed by a scream.

Emily and Sara ran to Kate. Sara clutched the hem of Kate's dress. Kate reached down to stop her sister's grasp from damaging the thin fabric, then stopped. She offered Sara her hand instead, but Sara clung tighter and sucked her thumb.

'Mummy's mad. Is she mad at us?'

'No, Emily. She's just tired.'

Daniel shook his head. 'She's mad bout *evryfing*.'

Kate didn't argue. Three pairs of eyes were fixed on her. She must stay calm. They needed her.

Settling the two girls onto the lower steps, she waited. Waited to see if the noise they'd heard was the beginning, or the end. It was never the middle of trouble.

Sara clung tighter to Kate's dress.

Kate wished she had jeans like the other girls. Carrie Evans even had embroidered flowers on the pockets of her jeans. It would be wonderful to pick out clothes. Not in the rushed way she had to buy food at the small grocery store with prying eyes watching her every move.

It was silent in the kitchen. Mother must have gone back to bed. Or the lounge room. If she had stayed in the kitchen the noise wouldn't have stopped. It was a bad sign.

'I'd better check dinner.'

Sara's anxious hands pawed at her dress, but this time she worked them free.

'You don't want dinner to burn, do you?'

Three solemn faces looked back. Emily shook her head.

'You go, Kate. Okay.'

Emily's back stiffened. Kate sighed. Her younger sister was learning to protect herself.

Emily put a hand on Sara's shoulder. 'Don't suck your thumb, Sara. You're not a baby.'

Sara slowly removed her thumb. 'You're not our mother. Kate is.'

Emily looked sharply at her young sister.

'Kate is not our mother. Mummy is.'

The smell of burning came from the open window of the kitchen. Kate jumped up.

'Don't fight children. It will be all right. Dad will be home soon.'

Daniel screwed up his face.

'Daddy can't cook, Kate. Even Bob knows that.'

The kitchen was silent. Kate had no time to look for her mother. The potatoes had begun to burn on the bottom of the pan. It would take her some time to scrape the dark charcoal. She would have to rescue the potatoes somehow. Tossing them quickly out of the pan into the colander, she rinsed them over and over. She placed a small piece of the crumbly flesh into her mouth. The potatoes tasted burned.

Hot tears stung her cheeks. No amount of salt or butter would disguise the taste.

One of the gas burners glowed, but there was nothing on it. The frozen vegetables sat in another saucepan, still cold.

Dinner was ruined.

The hall clock struck 6 o'clock. Kate wiped her tears with the edge of the tea towel. Usually by now, the children would have finished dinner and the tidying up would be done, leaving her with the simple task of warming her father's meal when he came home.

A key turned in the lock. Dad was home. Kate heard a rustling sound as her mother went to the door.

~~~

Three

> *Another way of expressing the head/heart conflict is our adult self as opposed to our 'inner child'.*

'Have you been drinking, Ellen?' Dad's voice was low, weary.

'No, Bruce. Of course not. I just rinsed my mouth...' pleading.

'Don't lie to me, Ellen. Where are the children?'

Mother began to cry, soft simpering sounds.

'I've had a terrible day. The children have been so loud. You don't know what it's like. After all those work dos for your company ... all those years...'

Kate's stomach formed a familiar tense knot. With trembling fingers she tried to finish the dinner preparations without making a sound.

She heard the thud of Dad's boots as they hit the floor. In her mind's eye, she could see her mother clinging to the front of her father's shirt.

'Bruce, please. I'm so bone tired.'

Kate cringed at the sound of her mother's desperate pleading.

'Face it, Ellen. You're depressed again. Are you taking your medication? You can't keep doing this. It's not fair on me, on the children. It's not a trade-off, Ellen. You have bipolar. You can't spend your life waiting for the highs.'

The soft thunk of her father's footsteps was joined by the pat-pat of her mother's bare feet. Closer.

'Why is Kate cooking dinner again Ellen? She's only ten for God's sake! What the hell have you been doing? Nothing! All day, and nothing!'

Father was yelling now.

Mother's hand was raised in front of her as if to push back the words, push back truth itself.

'You make me want to scream. Do you know you make me want to do that Bruce? That you push me so far? So close to the edge?'

Mother tore at her hair.

The back screen door squeaked. Emily, Daniel and Sara stood huddled in the doorway.

Kate froze.

She must stop this—this jarring of words. This sting. She must.

Any words would do.

'The wall is blue.'

~~~

Mother stopped screaming. Father stared at Kate. Then he saw Emily, Daniel and Sara.

'Go and have your baths children.'

His voice was low, defeated.

Tea was a miserable affair with Mother crying pitifully in the bedroom. The children pushed their food around, except for Kate who chattered cheerfully, overbright.

'Bob doesn't like burned potato mash.'

Daniel sneezed at the pepper Kate had put on his potatoes to mask the taste.

Father thumped the table.

'This is rubbish. It's inhuman. No man should have to live with this nonsense. I'm going out. Tell your mother if she doesn't make a doctor's appointment ... oh hell. Tell her I'm not coming back.'

The front door slammed. The car tyres spun gravel. Kate choked back tears as she comforted the others.

Mother came into the kitchen and began to bustle around. She put on her best apron. She filled the sink with sudsy water. She turned the radio on full blast.

'Your father's a pig!'

Kate helped the children with their baths and listened to Emily read. Daniel sobbed. 'Bob doesn't want to be on his own tonight. He's afraid.'

Kate held him. 'You and Bob can sleep with us. In our room. But he must be quiet.'

Daniel smiled.

~~~

The moon was low in the sky. Kate could see its comforting roundness from her bed, where Daniel lay tucked under her arm. He had stopped trying to make room beside him for Bob and had curled into his sister.

Kate knew she should try to sleep. Tomorrow would be full of buses and classes. And housework.

Mother had cleaned the kitchen for hours, long after Dad had come home. They had no words left then. No fight to interrupt with silly sentences about blue walls.

The wall clock struck twelve times. Midnight. Kate loved the wall clock. It seemed the only pretty thing in an ugly ordinary house. It didn't chime like other clocks. Each hour had a different birdsong.

She called it the birdsong clock, but told no one of the name she'd given it.

Once she had written about it in English at school and the teacher had asked a lot of questions, so she didn't mention the birdsong clock again.

The midnight breeze played with the yellowed curtains. They didn't look faded and old in the moonlight. They shone as if the magic of night could make everything different. Fluttering to their own song, the thin gauze fabric danced.

Kate wondered if there was a place where people had their own music like the birdsong clock. A separate rhythm for every living creature. Something no one else heard, or knew. Something that wouldn't change.

A song that belonged to her and no one else.

~~~

Four

*Everyone's journey is to shed the roles we think
define who we are.*

Kate would never have ventured into Mrs Wentworth's yard if Daniel hadn't crept through the slatted wooden fence. He'd been kicking the palings with dull repetition, almost trancelike.

Two of the palings had given way and swung gingerly from the top rusty nail.

'I followed Bob,' he told Emily who scampered after him, her voice strident in the early Sunday morning air.

The paling flicked back with a loud clack.

'Stupid boy.' Emily latched a rough hand onto Daniel's arm.

Daniel wrenched free then, suddenly afraid, stood frozen in the yard.

Emily rushed at him and tripped over a garden hose. 'Daniel! Stupid, silly bumhead!' She stood, picked at grass that clung to her knee and climbed back through the fence.

Kate carefully moved the paling aside. 'Daniel. Come back.'

Daniel didn't blink.

Sara tugged on Kate's legging with sticky fingers.

'Mind Sara, Emily.'

The second paling gave way with a heavy clunk as Kate squeezed through the gap.

'Daniel, you shouldn't be here.'

'Look Katie.'

A large ginger tabby washed its face, licking a paw then stroking it over an ear, head bent to the task, eyes closed.

Kate unfurled toes accustomed to tense retreat from bindies and placed a gentle hand on Daniel's shoulder. 'Oh, the grass is so soft.' She looked down at the thick bladed luxury. Forgetting where and why she was there she picked a wispy dandelion clock and blew it away.

Daniel watched, fascinated. He picked one, but dropped it when the milky fluid from the stem leaked onto his fingers.

'Do you like dandelions?' Mrs Wentworth stood holding pruning shears and smiling.

'They're yukky. Your cat is fat.' Daniel pointed at the ginger moggie who was winding itself around Daniel's leg.

'You can pick him up if you like. His name is Pudding.' The old woman wiped the back of a hand across her forehead. 'You're Daniel aren't you?'

Kate tensed.

'Yes.' Daniel scooped the cat up and was rewarded with a feline head-butt. He giggled. 'Hello Pudding.'

'We shouldn't be here.' Kate retreated, covering the burn on her arm with an anxious hand.

'I like your cat, Missers.' Daniel patted the animal's head.

'Let me look at that arm.' The old woman took off her gardening gloves.

'It's okay. I'm clumsy. I was cook...'

'What are you children doing? Kate?' Mother. Stretched to see over the fence. 'Hello, Margaret. I hope the children aren't being a nuisance.'

'Not at all, Ellen. They're just getting acquainted with Pudding.'

'I don't like them having sweets before meals.' Mother's face puckered.

Kate put both arms behind her back, hoping Mother hadn't seen the old lady inspecting the burn.

The old woman laughed. 'Pudding is the name of the cat, Ellen. He's taken quite a shine to your Daniel. And that's something. He doesn't usually like children.'

Kate's mouth went dry. She moved towards Daniel who held the cat tightly.

'Put the cat down, Daniel.' Mother grew taller, on tiptoes.

'I. Don't. Want. To.' Daniel curled his bottom lip. 'Bob wants a cat. Mummy, please?'

'You'd better come home now, children.' Mother's voice was pinched tight. She pointed to the side gate at the front of Mrs Wentworth's house. 'Don't forget to the shut the gate on your way. Now!'

Kate glanced at the fence. The paling had swung back. Mother hadn't noticed.

Mrs Wentworth walked with them to the gate, smiling a plump-cheeked smile, chatting. Clicking the gate ajar, she paused. 'Come anytime, Kate. It's just an old fence.'

Kate thought she saw the old woman wink but it probably only the sun in her eyes.

That afternoon as Kate was helping the younger ones pick up their outside toys she found a tube of burn ointment at the base of the fence near the loose paling.

She snatched it up, shoving it deep in her pocket.

Mother spent three months in bed, sinking deeper into the fug of depression. She'd finally allowed Father to take her back to the doctor.

He organised regular deliveries of plastic casing packs called Webster Packs, filled with bright pills. The days of the week were written, even the weekend days, then *Breakfast, Lunch, Tea, Night.*

Zoe, the chemist girl, delivered them every week on Thursdays. Father put them in one of his drawers. Kate saw him looking at them, running a slim finger over the

the wall is blue

days, back and forth as if to reassure himself. He'd sigh and close the drawer, turning a key in the lock. It must be kept from small prying fingers. Mother couldn't be counted on to guarantee that.

At first Father had to prop her up in the bed to take them, in the morning and at night. Then she waved him aside and told him not to get up so early, just for her.

Then Mother started getting up again, wandering loosely around the house in her dressing gown. She even accepted a peck on the cheek from Father and tolerated brief hugs from Daniel and Sara. Emily stood back, eyes grim and detached. Kate had stopped a long time ago.

Mother had no tight words anymore, just quiet, dull ones. Words without meaning, acquiescing, sometimes pleading.

For a week she'd prepared tea. It was the same thing every night, frozen veg and steak. No one said anything. Their words were hidden among the solemn rustling of the pause of days.

It was like a pause on the edge of something. Would it be up or down? It was too soon to tell.

~~~

The children didn't mention the loose palings. Daniel least of all. Visits in search of the marmalade cat were too important.

Mrs Wentworth seemed to be in the yard more often.

Or when she was, she made a point of saying hello to the children and waving at their Mother.

Mother began doing the washing.

Father didn't have to rush around at night after work piling load after load into the washer, then the dryer. With Kate helping.

He had time to read the day's paper at the table after tea.

Then one Sunday morning Mother hung the washing on the line. Kate sat out the back with one eye on the book she was reading while Daniel and Sara rushed through the sheets and clothes. She wished they wouldn't do it. She tensed every time one of them grabbed a sheet.

'Don't pull on those, Daniel and Sara.' Kate put her book down and tried to get them interested in another game.

Mother didn't seem worried when she came out with another load. She even had a few words with Mrs Wentworth over the fence. 'She's just a lonely old thing.' Mother said, as she flicked the iron over a shirt.

Kate, holding a coat hanger, waiting for the next garment, was stunned. Lonely? Were adults lonely too?

'Hang this up in your father's wardrobe.' After their angry fight, Kate's mother had been subdued. She'd spoken carefully to her husband. He, in turn, was polite. Their faces and voices had no expression, as if they were too weary; the air in the room too heavy to move against.

Kate returned from hanging the shirts.

'Why don't you take the children over to Mrs Wentworth's? She's been asking if you'd like to go.'

'What?' Kate stilled.

The three younger children didn't hesitate.

While Emily, Daniel and Sara sat on the floor, diving into a basket of old toys, Mrs Wentworth sat Kate at the kitchen table and put a waterproof dressing on her arm.

'Hot chocolate for all.' Mrs Wentworth flicked the kettle on. 'Next time—cupcakes!'

'Cupcakes!' shrieked the three.

'Next time,' whispered Kate. What delicious words.

~~~

It was Kate's last year of primary school. She'd be leaving the younger ones behind. The kids at school talked of end-of-year ceremonies and end-of-school celebrations. Kate would soon turn twelve.

"Wednesday next week is Grandparent Day!!!" Kate's teacher wrote on the blackboard. Miss Lawson favoured coloured chalks, and wrote the way she taugh. Her fast, scratching movements swirled rainbow dusting that puffed then fell to the dull grey carpet. Sometimes her writing was so energetic the chalk broke.

Grandparents. Kate hadn't thought about them in a long time. Father's mother was in a nursing home in Queensland. Mother's parents were a mystery to Kate.

She had vague memories of fruity perfume, rough whiskered chins and musty woollen coats.

Kate sucked on her teeth and shoved books into her backpack. A large ceiling fan slowly shifted humid air around the room. Kate felt nausea rise and fought it.

She was sure everyone in the class had at least one grandparent and many probably had four. It was hard enough to make and keep friends when she couldn't invite them home anytime she liked. She'd really stand out if she had no grandparent to bring.

The school day was nearly over. Kate twisted in her chair towards the door, one hand clutched her backpack. She couldn't wait to leave.

She couldn't pretend to be sick. Emily, Daniel and Sara needed her to help get them ready.

'We don't have grandparents.' Adnan spoke with a rolling accent. He was a Syrian refugee, a talkative, dark-haired child who protected his shy twin sister, Lely. 'Not here. They still live in Al-Hasakah, in my old country. And they...'

'That's okay, Adnan. Do you have an aunt or uncle? A sponsor?'

'Oh yes, Miss. We have Mrs Depford. She's been in Australia a very long time. Actshally, she was born here.'

Miss Lawson was quick to respond. Adnan was inclined to tell long involved stories, unlike his sister Lely who blushed and preferred to speak in Arabic, usually through her brother.

'Wonderful, Adnan. She's welcome. It doesn't matter that she's not related to you.' Miss Lawson dusted chalk off her hands and looked around the classroom. 'That goes for anyone else. Some of you might have grandparents who are too far away to come.'

On the way home, sitting alone on the school bus, Kate thought of Mrs Wentworth as light fingers traced the deep crack in the vinyl bench seat beside her. The old woman was kind, she kept secrets and slipped small things through the gap in the paling fence. And best of all, Kate often had a brief respite in the afternoons before Daniel and Sara were dropped off by Mrs Blakehurst.

Emily, now ten, preferred to watch telly at home. Father had brought home a small television that he'd placed in the sunroom at the back so the children wouldn't disturb their mother.

Mrs Wentworth. Was it too much to hope that she'd like to come to Grandparents Day? Kate stared out of the bus window. The shrieks of the other children jarred more than usual. It was easier to cope with constant disappointment than deal with hope, a commodity that was always deliciously out of reach. And there were so many things she could hope for, if only she'd let herself. All of the end of year celebrations, especially the school concert. Kate sang in the choir, a guilty pleasure.

The driver threatened to report Billy Dawson, who

was standing on a seat pelting the children behind him with Twisties. Kate noticed that the boy who often tried to speak to her was perched on the end of her seat. He hugged his backpack as if he was trying to be as inconspicuous as possible. He gave Kate a shy smile and edged even further towards the edge of the seat, nearly toppling in the aisle.

A tram rattled past, clattering on the tracks, never early or late. Kate glimpsed Mrs Wentworth who waved an umbrella at Kate, and smiled. I'll do it, Kate decided. If Mrs Wentworth said yes, Mother would have to agree. It would be Kate's first small act of rebellion. The anticipation was euphoric, but only for a moment.

~~~

Mother wasn't at home when Kate arrived. Emily went straight to the sunroom. Soon cartoons blared.

Kate made anxious circles in the dining room, tensed for every sound. She rehearsed sentences, phrases, editing words, so preoccupied she was shocked when Daniel and Sara rushed through the front door. 5:30. Mother was very late.

They left the door open. Mrs Blakehurst waited on the doorstep. She smiled.

'Oh dear, it's Thursday isn't it!' Kate fumbled in the hallway drawer. The envelope with Mrs Blakehurst's pay wasn't there.

the wall is blue

Kate's face burned.

'Never mind, pet.' Mrs Blakehurst patted Kate's shoulder. 'Some other time will be fine.'

~~~

Mother arrived at 7pm, carrying bags of Kentucky Fried Chicken.

'Indoor picnic time children,' she announced, sending Emily to the car to bring in drinks.

Kate stalled. Mother usually sent her to the car. Was she hiding something?

Emily, Daniel and Sara squealed with delight. Mother spread a tablecloth on the lounge room floor and joined the younger ones in a riotous party. Kate was too angry to speak. It wouldn't have made any difference. Mother was buzzing like a bee in springtime giddy on nature's bounty.

'Come on, Kate. Hurry up and have something to eat. Your father will be home soon. He'll be mad as hell if he knows we've had take-away for tea. Don't you tell, children.'

Emily, Daniel and Sara giggled. No, they wouldn't tell.

'Daddy won't get mad.' Kate spat the words at her mother. Mother didn't notice. Kate grabbed a chicken drumstick and nibbled it at the edge of the "picnic". She wondered how both parents could possess a seemingly endless ability to accuse the other of crimes.

'Oops, nearly forgot!' Mother clapped a hand over her mouth, ran to the car and returned, loaded with shopping bags from departments stores. There were fancy blue and silver shopping bags with ribbon handles and adorned with elegant women.

Kate opened the hallway drawer and pointed. She wouldn't accuse in front of Emily, Daniel and Sara.

'Don't look at me like that Kate Stone. A woman deserves a few luxuries in life. Anyway, I've got a job. So there! I'm going to be a rep for a confectionary company.'

Mother threw bags of lollies on the floor.

~~~

Mother was perfumed, dressed and out of the house before the children had eaten their breakfast. Off to her next job, as excited as if she'd won the lottery. Emily had an excursion and was picked up by a friend's mother. Mrs Blakehurst collected Daniel and Sara.

Kate cleared the table, more slowly than usual. She stared at the birdsong clock. She'd leave at the 8:15 chime. But the chime came and went. And still Kate sat on the lounge chair. She heard the school bus grind its gears past the house. She heard the postman's bike and the ting of the letterbox. She heard Mrs Wentworth watering the garden.

Kate put her dressing gown over her uniform, slipped

through the gap in the paling fence. She had lunch with Mrs Wentworth. The old woman was honoured to be invited to Grandparents' Day. Kate told Mrs Wentworth she was sick. She told her that Mother was pleased she was inviting the neighbour to a school event.

Mrs Wentworth didn't believe a word of either claim. She offered Kate another biscuit and vowed not to mention any of the conversation to Kate's mother.

~~~

'This is my neighbour, Mrs Wentworth,' Kate said, smiling on Grandparent's Day.

Mrs Wentworth gave a talk about working in David Jones at the cosmetic counter in the main Sydney store. The children laughed as she told them stories of meeting movie stars who she'd helped buy perfume for their wives. The class asked questions and Mrs Wentworth answered them. Kate was so proud of Mrs Wentworth she almost forgot she was a pretend grandparent.

Kate didn't tell her mother. She was learning to keep secrets from her.

~~~

Five

> *Significant losses may stay buried, but they will surface somewhere, sometime.*

A period of calm descended on the Stone home. At least for Kate and the children. She had time to stretch out in the autumn cool, luxuriate in the shade of the Crepe Myrtle tree. She treasured these moments, wanting them to be endless.

Mother relished her job, working long hours going from store to store. Father smiled a lot more, although Kate overheard him talking to a golf buddy. 'Ellen's on the up again. God help us all.'

The money for Mrs Blakehurst was always in the hallway drawer.

The garden flourished with new buds and bees under Father's care and Mother seemed to catch the buzz. She was a woman reborn.

When she wasn't working she baked and cleaned. She made cupcakes and brownies, slices and sweets. The children were a little delirious with joy, and perhaps an excess of sugar. Even when the Tupperware containers were full, and the fridge and freezer overflowed, still Mother kept going.

Father didn't relax. 'It's a bad sign.'

Kate understood a little of his attitude. She was old enough to remember the cycle of things. The younger ones revelled in the calm, and she let them. If they noticed that Kate no longer prepared school lunches and dinners, they did not say. After all, the bounty of cake every day was not to be questioned, but celebrated.

Mother had begun to experiment with recipes for Kate's 12th birthday party. She claimed it would be the best party ever. There were pieces of paper taped all over the fridge.

But then she started doing odd things. Kate found unopened tins in the kitchen bin. She returned them to the cupboard and said nothing.

Mother insisted on having the key to the tablet drawer. Then pills started appearing, carelessly fallen into the cracks in the laundry tiles. Father found them first, then warned Kate and Emily to watch out for them with the younger ones.

Kate didn't want a party. It was too hard to make friends with children she'd been too busy to spend time with before. Too ashamed to ask home.

'I don't want any fuss, Mum.' Kate had stopped calling her Mummy.

'Don't be silly, pet. All your friends will be disappointed. Think how excited they'll be.' Mother hummed and danced around the kitchen. 'I want you to make a list—all your friends, Kate. All of them.'

But Kate didn't want to think about that. She wished there was a way to stop the party. Maybe she could lose the invitations. Not that there would be many. She was avoiding the subject of the list.

'Dad.'

'Yes, pet.'

'I don't really want a birthday party.'

Dad took off his glasses and put down the newspaper. 'I understand.'

He rested his head on the back of the chair, and sighed. 'Your Aunt Isabelle is coming.'

'Really! Oh, that's wonderful. We haven't seen her for years. I would love her at a party. If I must have one. Maybe she can talk Mum into a family party. Why is she coming?'

'She's coming to help your mother.'

'Is ... Mum ... all right, Dad?'

'She's manic, love.'

Kate's forehead creased. 'What's manic mean?'

Rather pinched the bridge of his nose. 'It's a part of Mummy's disease.'

Kate's eyes widened. 'Is Mum sick?'

'Not sick precisely. She has bipolar. It's sort of ... a

mood disease. It means she has very low times and then very high moods. She goes from one to the other and back again.'

Kate considered this. 'She's in the high bit now, isn't she?'

'Yes, pet.'

'And she was in the really low bit a couple of years ago when I had to...'

'Yes, pet.'

Kate's father patted the sofa beside him. Kate glanced at the door. Mother was in the kitchen singing along with the radio.

A tear pricked at the corner of Kate's eye. 'Can they make her better? The doctors? Someone?'

Father chewed on his bottom lip. 'They ... they've tried. There are tablets that can help, they even out the high times and the low times. But ... well, your mother doesn't take them, she doesn't like them. Except when she's really sad.'

'The low bits?'

'Yes, Kate. The low bits.'

'But why doesn't she take them if they make her better? I don't understand. Do they taste really yukky?' Kate's voice rose, then she remembered Mother in the kitchen and looked down.

Father continued. 'She says they make her feel different. Not like herself. She doesn't like the low times—

she hates that. But, it's hard for us to understand. I don't. I get mad, and take it out on you kids. And then I'm sorry because it's not your fault that she's like this. I yell and try to make her understand what she'd doing to us all, but that makes things worse.'

'So you go out?'

Father put his head in his hands. 'I'm sorry Kate.'

'But ... but, the tablets, and how they make her feel can't be worse than this, this high and low stuff. It's horrible. Why would anyone put up with all that up and down?'

Kate damped down her distress, she wanted so badly to understand. If she got too upset Dad would stop explaining, and she didn't want him to stop because it was the first time he'd talked about it.

Maybe Mother was like a jigsaw puzzle they could put back together. Maybe she'd do it for love. If only she knew how much it meant to them all. For her to be better; to be really with them.

'Your mother likes the high feeling, she says it makes her feel wonderful, more alive than anything else. She says she feels closer to us all, closer to everything in the universe. She feels she can do anything—like being a superhero.'

Kate frowned. 'But superheroes aren't real, Dad.'

'I know, Kate, but your mother...'

'Why can't she see? She's in the high bit now—but

what use is it? She's only cooking cakes, we can't live on cake. She cleans the same things over and over again. She talks rubbish to people in the street. That's not more alive, it's crazy. She drives fast and waves to people, everybody, even policemen—why only last week she got three fines ... oh, dear, I wasn't supposed to tell.'

Father looked shocked, then angry. *'Ellen!'*

~~~

That was one of the worst fights. Mother had more energy and screamed louder. Father told her off for hurting the family, the children, and him. He yelled that he wished he'd never met her. That it would serve her right if the kids turned out as nuts as she was.

One thing was different though. Mother left in the car, not Father. The revving engine and the gravel made the same sound. The desolation was the same.

Kate went into the kitchen. Some of the dishes and cakes were smashed and the children were crying, again. She would have her wish. There would be no birthday celebration.

~~~

Six

> *Anyone can be a valuable presence in the life of a hurting person. All we need to do is sit and listen, really listen with our heart.*

Aunt Isabelle was Father's sister. She arrived with a cheery smile and a shiny silver suitcase.

Mother was angry. She greeted her sister-in-law in a cool voice, then walked away leaving Father to settle his sister in the sunroom. She called Kate to help her with the cooking.

'What's wrong, Mum?'

'Why did your father ask his sister, and not mine? He wants her to check up on me. He'd like to lock me away. Kate, you must be my eyes and ears. If your father and Aunt Isabelle...'

Aunt Isabelle came into the kitchen.

If she had heard any of what Mother said, she didn't show it in any way. Patting Kate on the head, she began to dry the dishes.

'The children can do that. They don't need you doing

their chores.' Mother's voice was quick and sharp.

'That's fine, Ellen. I just like to pull my weight.' Aunt Isabelle kept drying the plates.

'Why are you here anyway, Isabelle? Did Bruce put you up to this?'

Mother slapped the dishcloth into the sink.

'Oh, Ellen, I didn't come to make trouble. It seems that Bruce didn't tell you I was coming. I'm so sorry. I can stay at a hotel if it makes things easier.'

Aunt Isabelle hung the tea towel carefully on the railing in the under-sink cupboard.

'Don't mind me, Isabelle. I'm ... I'm not myself at the moment. Things have been such a struggle. Of course I don't want you to leave...'

Aunt Isabelle smiled and hugged Mother.

'It's okay, Ellen. I thought while I was here you and I could have some time together.'

Tears sprung to Mother's eyes.

'I would love that. I'm so silly. Take no notice of me.'

She laughed and wiped the tears with her apron. 'It's a shame you missed Kate's 12th birthday last year. We had a wonderful party. She's in high school now, you know.'

~~~

Kate went outside.

With her back against the rough bark of the Crepe Myrtle she curled up and faced away from the children.

Wrapping her arms around her knees she leant her head into the circle of that solitary embrace. Her heart cried out for voice.

For the first time Kate's feelings towards her mother turned to anger. It was an emotion that had no place before. No space within. The memory of her mother's words stung. *'We had a wonderful party.'*

How could Mother lie?

She was angry with herself too. She'd been part of the lie. She **had** wanted a party. She **had** wanted friends. But most of all she wanted a normal family.

Kate shrank into the centre of herself, moving to the dark shadowed corner between the tree and the fence. It was cool and quiet there, but not even the sounds of Mrs Wentworth cooing to the birds as she fed them soothed her.

She cupped her hands over her ears. The noise of the children playing faded into the background. She didn't want to mind the children today, she didn't even want to talk to them.

If wishes came true, and of course none of them ever did, she would be invisible. As invisible as she was to the grownups.

~~~

Daniel walked towards the tree.

'Kate! Bob wants a drink. He's thirsty. Can't we go

inside? Why aren't you getting tea for us?'

Kate moved to the other side. Out of sight.

Sara's little legs pounded a rhythm to where Kate sat. 'Kate! Kate! Daniel wants you!'

Hot tears scalded Kate's eyes and ran down her cheek. She looked up at Daniel and Sara.

Emily left her skipping and came to investigate. She saw Kate's tearstained face and turned shocked eyes on her sister.

Kate let the tears run unheeded. She didn't care who saw her tears, her pain—not anymore. She was a child. She wasn't a grownup.

Emily began to whimper.

Mother came running down the stairs.

'Kate ... darling.' Mother reached out but Kate drew back.

Kate's eyes burned. Her hands trembled.

'Why did you tell Aunt Isabelle I had a birthday party? Why did you lie?'

Mother turned and saw Isabelle poised on the top step. She flushed bright red. Isabelle turned and went back up the stairs. Emily, Daniel and Sara stood frozen. This was a new drama.

Mother looked at the ground. 'Why darling, I didn't know a party was so important.'

She stumbled over the words and smoothed her hair.

Kate stood, fists clenched at her sides.

the wall is blue

'It wasn't the party! Don't you understand anything! It was a lie! That's what's important!'

~~~

'Bob wants a drink!'

Daniel's voice held an edge of panic. His eyes were wide. Kate had never talked to Mother like that.

Emily's voice was sharp. 'Bob isn't real, you silly boy. You're too old for an invisible friend. You'll be at school next year...'

Kate gasped.

When had Mother's words started to come out of Emily's mouth?

~~~

Mother made a special effort for tea, or perhaps it was for Aunt Isabelle. There were pretty paper serviettes—the ones Mother had bought for Kate's party.

Kate's throat tightened. She pushed her food around the plate.

The cracked plastic tablecloth with the faded roses had been replaced by a red check linen tablecloth. Mother's hair was coiled up. Father had arrived home on time and brought milk and bread. Mother smiled a lot.

'Thank you, Bruce. That's very thoughtful.'

It was their first evening meal together since Aunt Isabelle had arrived. The grownups didn't seem to know what to say, all talking at once, then muted silence. Words jerking and stalling.

'This is lovely. We should have visitors for tea more often.' Mother realised what she'd said and fell silent.

'Nice tea, dear.' Father looked down as he spoke, then worked his way methodically through the food on his plate.

Kate couldn't remember a time when there had been anyone but their small family at a meal table. It was as if adding one person had changed everything. Apart from finding a place to sit, the whole evening was awkward. All the routines that fitted every other day were abandoned.

The brittle politeness made Kate tense. Everyone's role had changed. It was like a final rehearsal for a play with everyone realising how important it was to get things right, but worrying someone would forget their lines, or their place and everything would fall apart.

After tea Aunt Isabelle was allowed to help in the kitchen. Mother seemed to be best friends with her now, finishing the clearing up together and sharing a pot of tea. Before Kate could usher the children off for their baths, Father had taken charge.

~~~

Kate woke to the thrumming beat of heavy rain on the tin roof. No sound was heard above the din of the downpour. Kate revelled in the soothing cocoon it created. Her favourite kind of day.

Better still it was Sunday. No rush through puddles and potholes for buses or classes with Emily. No hurrying the little ones to the door for Mrs Blakehurst.

The first sound that penetrated the pouring rain was the sound of Aunt Isabelle and the children playing Rumicub. With a contended sigh Kate rolled over to face the wall. She loved the wallpaper. Apparently Father and Mother had laughed and played as they applied the whimsical Alice in Wonderland paper. Even though it was peeling in places it still held magic for Kate.

She drifted off to sleep, lost down the rabbit hole with Alice in a world where children had power over their destiny, power over evil queens and where childhood nonsense not only had a place, but was par for the course.

Later in the day when Mother was watching television with the youngest children and Father was mowing the lawn, Aunt Isabelle took Kate and Emily to the shopping centre. She bought gifts for Daniel and Sara with excited advice from the girls.

'Now Kate, Emily, what can I buy for you?'

Kate worried her bottom lip, but Emily had no hesitation. 'Ooh, I'd love a new backpack and lunchbox for school. Don't dig me in the ribs, Kate!'

'Fine—now Kate?'

'She's been hanging out for a new pair of jeans. You should see the way she...'

'Right, new jeans it is.' Aunt Isabelle smiled.

~~~

Thrilled with their presents and eager to share their happiness with the younger children, Kate and Emily ran through the door when they arrived home.

It was eerily quiet. They went from room to room, becoming more anxious by the minute. Even Aunt Isabelle's face was pale.

The house was empty.

The phone rang. It was Mrs Blakehurst. Mother had dropped the children off there.

~~~

Seven

> *It's so difficult for a person to be real with someone who isn't.*

Melanie Blakehurst leaned on the door of her husband's shed.

'Have you put the kids to bed, love? Rotten business.' Dave Blakehurst hung the last of his tools on the board of his shed wall. 'That young Daniel had a wonderful time in here. Guess he doesn't get out into his father's shed.'

'I think Bruce is more of a golf bloke than a shed guy.' Melanie was exhausted.

'Has he turned up yet?'

'Yes, he and Ellen are ... sorting things out now,' Melanie said. When Dave didn't respond, she continued. 'That's them screaming at each other.'

'Oh! Haven't heard a thing. That's not good. The sister must be upset about that. Izzy isn't it?'

'Isabelle, Izzy. She packed up and left. Ellen insisted.

Said she was causing trouble. She accused Dave of inviting his sister to show her up in front of the kids.'

'Ah women. Dave should've seen that coming.'

Melanie slapped his arm.

Dave grinned, snaked out a hand to slip her arm through his. 'Come inside, Melanie. I'll make you an Irish coffee.'

'How Irish?'

'Very Irish.'

'Better not be too Irish, I'll probably have to get up to one of the kids. I made Kate sleep in a room by herself. She already has too much responsibility.'

~~~

Kate stretched out in the guest room. She did angel wings like she'd seen people do in the movies in the snow, and still she couldn't feel the edges of the bed. The sheets were silky soft and smelled of lilies.

She'd never stayed at anyone's house before. Not even when Emily, Daniel and Sara were born.

Mrs Blakehurst had hugged her and told her to call her Auntie Melanie. That felt strange so she'd shaken her head. Everything felt odd, tilted.

She hadn't wanted to eat tea. Until she'd smelled the chicken schnitzels sizzling in the pan, seen the creamy smooth mashed potatoes and the beans cooked just right.

~~~

Eight

> *Enabling people to be real about themselves is an essential prerequisite to discovering real peace.*

That was the day Father left, for good.

Grownup conversations were whispered with sideways glances at the children. Where once Kate had been in the middle of all the grownup decisions, responsibilities and fights, she was now relegated to meagre facts.

Fuelled by anger Mother made quick, erratic decisions, pushing Kate aside. Kate should have been relieved, but she wasn't.

People came and went. Mother repelled them all, some swiftly, some slowly. She yelled at Father to leave the property whenever he came around.

After a few months Kate realised that Father had gone and somehow they must go on without him. Life became a march of dull shifting shadows. Now childhood was over for all the children, not just Kate.

~~~

Then the pendulum swung on its erratic course and Mother shrunk back to her bedroom. The children were all at school now.

Kate organised the delivery of the Webster Packs. Naturally this had to be done over the phone. The chemist girl delivered them every week. Kate put them in the bedside drawer her father had used. Kate checked them, back and forth, then turned the key in the lock. She helped her mother lean forward, swallow every bright pill, every dull buff pill and sip enough water.

Kate wore the key around her neck.

Emily, Daniel and Sara didn't need to know about this new duty of Kate's. They had enough, with school.

At first Kate had to prop Mother up in the bed to take them, in the morning and at night. Then, gradually Mother sat in the recliner Kate had moved into the bedroom. Emily and Daniel had tried to help but they'd been more nuisance than help so Kate had inched it down the hall and into the room. It was better than Mother spending all day and night in bed, staring at the ceiling.

For several weeks, or months at a time, Mother spent most of her time there, in a tattered, stained dressing gown that took all of Kate's time to take off her mother to wash.

the wall is blue

Then, like a bird taking flight in response to some mysterious inner siren call, Mother rose, went back to work, did the housework and shopping, carrying on as if nothing had been amiss.

~~~

Spring came, crisp and clean, skipping back to winter for days at a time, then forward to summer. Gone.

The seasons repeated their rhythmic cycles, again and again. Mother crashed and bumped between the world of mania and depression in her own erratic cycle, out of touch with Nature's rhyme.

II

Nine

Grief is the issue of the heart, not the head.

The cardiac monitor beeped erratically. Father looked pale and old connected to all the wires and tubes that snaked across the bed.

Emily clicked sleek red nails on the bedside table. 'I hate hospitals. How long has Dad had heart trouble, Kate? You could have told us, you know.'

The colour in Kate's cheeks rose. She paused as she arranged the dahlias in the vase with clean water.

'This is the first I've known, Emily. People have sudden heart attacks, you know.'

Emily folded her arms. 'But you're the one living at home, Kate. Though why you stayed beats me. You have to travel so far for your job.'

Father stirred and opened his eyes.

Daniel looked out of the huge glass hospital window, then turned to his father, clearing his throat nervously.

'Has Mum been in today, Dad? Er ... or y' girlfriend, Fiona?'

'Your mother was here this morning.' Father's voice was strained. His skin was grey, his cheeks sunken. He ran thin fingers through a few days' growth on a face too tender to permit shaving.

Emily flicked a thread from her suit. 'Don't tell us she was too *tired* to stay.'

Kate finished with the flowers, sat on the side of the bed and held his hand.

Emily pouted, then prodded Sara. 'You could at least pretend to be part of the family, Sara.'

Sara pulled one of the earplugs from her iPod.

'Pardon?'

Emily snorted. 'Ever the baby of the family.'

Daniel started pacing. Kate frowned at him but he didn't appear to notice. Finally he spoke.

'I'm no good at this sort of thing. Glad you're awake, Dad. Scared us half to death, old man.'

A nurse came in to take Father's observations and check the monitors. Emily, Daniel and Sara took the opportunity to offer brief goodbyes and leave. Kate frowned. Emily mouthed 'he left us'.

Kate chatted to the nurse and watched her ministrations with interest. Not that nursing was a profession that had any appeal. Her junior management position at an inner city hotel suited her down to the ground. She had started working there straight after Uni. Ben, her boyfriend had suggested it, confident of her abilities. They had worked on many projects together while they were students.

'You'd be great at it, Kate. It's not just reception work, but planning events and coordinating conventions. It would be great experience for our future ... if we ever decide to ... you know...'

Father looked sleepy, but the nurse reassured Kate she could stay. As she watched him drift off, she climbed into the spacious window seat and thought of Ben. How could they have a future? He hadn't pressured her, but he'd made it clear he wanted a life with her. He'd always been understanding about her mother and the care she needed. She was no longer able to work.

The hospital was a one storey building. It sprawled out; surrounded by narrow crowded garden beds. Kate looked for lilly pillies and saw none. The lawns were manicured. The staff had been wonderful. Kate had no complaints about public hospitals. Father couldn't afford anything else anyway.

~~~

'You've always been a good kid, Kate. A better daughter than I deserved.'

Kate turned surprised eyes to her father. The lips that had formed the words were a dusky blue.

'Thanks, Dad.'

He adjusted the nasal prongs for the oxygen. 'I'm dying, you know pet.'

'Yes Dad, I know.'

He laughed—a crackling sound. 'You always were the honest one.'

It was an effort for him to talk. He was breathless and every word took its toll.

'Your mother and Fiona think I have pneumonia. Don't know where they got that idea.'

Kate slipped down from her perch in the window seat and sat on his bed.

'That's what they choose to believe, Dad. It's what they need to think. Or want to; doesn't matter which.'

He coughed the cough of a drowning man.

Kate looked into his eyes. 'They told you then? The doctors?'

'Congestive Cardiac Failure. Kidneys out of whack too. Fiona won't have a bar of it. Keeps pushing for asthma stuff and adrenaline. Watches too much telly.'

Kate gave a wry smile.

'She's a bit like Mum.'

'S'pose so.'

A nurse entered. She was generously curved in a womanly way. A real woman. Her skin was flawless. Kate wondered at her secret.

Father winked. 'Easy on the eye this one.'

The nurse smiled indulgently.

'Well, Mr Stone. I have some medication for you. It's a diuretic to get rid of some of that fluid in your lungs and make your breathing more comfortable.'

She produced a syringe from a kidney dish and administered the medication via the IV cannula.

Father rolled his eyes.

'How will that help when I'll be peeing every five minutes?'

He raised a weak hand.

'We're going to put a catheter in.'

'But...'

'No buts, Mr Stone.'

Father slumped back on the pillows, exhausted.

'Kate...'

'Just rest Dad.'

She distracted him by describing the scene outside the window until he closed his eyes. Then she picked up the newspaper and started filling in the crossword puzzle, while chewing the end of the pen. A childhood habit.

She was just finishing it half an hour or so later when she felt her father's eyes on her.

'Kate.'

'Yes, Dad.'

Father's gaze was intense. 'Your fella—what's his name?'

'Ben.'

'Choose him. Not this.'

Kate's eyes clouded. What did he mean? This?

'Have your own life. Home and happiness. The others tease you about still living at home, but you're doing it for your mother.'

Kate felt a rush of anger. 'But who's going to...'

'Your mother can stay with Melanie Blakehurst. Board with her and have regular check-ups.'

'Mrs Blakehurst? You've already...'

Her father held up a hand.

'When you're ready, Kate. Melanie is the closest to being a friend to your mother since I've known her.'

Father paused. 'I know I don't have the right...'

'No, you don't.'

'Just think about it. That's all I ask. Melanie understands better than most. If you're not there propping your mother up, she'll have to get real help. I don't mean just medication. She might get some counselling. I know I stuffed up. I didn't cope ... You deserve ... more.'

Kate relented her stiff pose. 'It's not that easy, Dad.'

'Think about it. Promise me you'll do that.'

'Okay, I will. I'm sorry for being prickly. You didn't give up on us, not really. You stayed close by, and ... you've still helped with Mum.'

Kate remembered regular child support payments. He wasn't a wealthy man, but he'd never missed. He'd even helped out with the rent sometimes, or food.

She liked Fiona, in a sort of fashion. It was to her credit that she'd never pulled their father away or complained about his responsibilities. In fact, Kate suspected she thought more of him for it.

'Your mother did her best with what she had, Kate. I hope you know that.'

Tears fell silently down Kate's cheeks.

'I know, Dad. I love her. I know how hard things are for her. I worry that I might...'

'Have it?'

'Yes.' It was such a relief to say that one word.

Her father stretched out his hand and pulled her down for an embrace. 'You're twenty eight, pet. I don't think you have much to worry about. There are usually signs in the early twenties.'

'Really?'

Father stroked her back. 'Don't live in the shadow of fear, pet. See a doctor, or a counsellor. Wouldn't hurt. It might help understand your mother. Don't take it all on yourself. Just because the others...'

A nurse came in after a gentle tap in the door and busied herself with the chart at the end of the bed.

Father picked up a small key. His fumbled attempts to fit it in the keyhole showed his frailty.

Kate took it and opened the drawer.

'What are you looking for, Dad?'

Reaching in, he found a piece of paper. It was a

nursing chart page he must have cadged from one of the nurses.

'Turn it over, Kate.'

Kate squinted to read the words above her father's scrawled signature.

The birdsong clock belongs to Kate Stone.

Ten

> *Let the wounded teach us what it's like for them; making them and their pain of value to us.*

'Come in Kate. I gather you've had a chat with your dad.' Mrs Blakehurst ushered Kate inside.

'Yes, I did, Mrs Blakehurst.'

'It's high time you called me Melanie. Or Aunt Melanie if you're more comfortable.'

They sat at the dining room table where Kate and the others had often chatted over milk and cookies. Mrs Blakehurst fussed over the tea service and brought the biscuit jar.

'Dad made me think about a few things.'

'He's a good man, really.'

Mrs Blakehurst poured the tea. 'I hope you'll think about it. You're not giving up on your mother by letting go of her daily care and moving on with your own life. There will be many things in place for her here with me.

Your father has always kept an eye on her, but...'

'I know Dad hasn't got long. He probably won't come home from hospital.' Kate sighed.

'His father had heart trouble and died young.'

'Oh, I didn't know that. As if I need another thing to worry about facing later in life.'

'You poor love.' Mrs Blakehurst laughed. 'We've all got to go sometime. The important thing is to learn to live before we die.'

'I guess.'

Caesar, Mrs Blakehurst's Spaniel whimpered at the dog door, his eyes pleading with his mistress.

'Oh really, Caesar. You can get through the door yourself. You're as autocratic as a cat.'

She went to the sliding door and opened it. Caesar rewarded her with muddy paws and sloppy kisses.

'Your mother will be all right, Kate. What about your future?'

'Well I love my job...'

Caesar transferred his attention to Kate, leaping onto her lap and gazing up at her.

'That's all very well, but what of love? What about taking care of you? It's your first responsibility, you know.'

'Funny, that's what Ben says.'

Mrs Blakehurst laughed. 'Wise young man. Plan on keeping him?'

Kate beamed. 'Oh yes. In fact, I'm going there next.'

Mrs Blakehurst pulled the biscuits away from Kate. 'Then why are you wasting time here? Skedaddle.'

Kate knocked hesitantly on the door of Ben's apartment. Her heart was racing. Ben opened the door and pulled her to him.

'How did you hear my soft tapping, Ben Wright?'

'I have exceptional hearing, my love.'

'That's good, because I have something to say.'

Ben stood and kissed her forehead with patient tenderness. 'I'm listening.'

Kate's voice trembled. 'I choose you, Ben. And I choose me.'

Bipolar disorder
(Steele Fitchett)

Bipolar sufferers have a large variation in their experiences. Not only is there a great range of symptoms, but also there is no typical picture that describes those who find themselves with this diagnosis.

~~~

The person who taught me so much about the bipolar condition was Andrew, a very bright young man in his early thirties.

For him, the experience of going 'high' gave such exhilaration, and coming 'down' (to what the rest of us call normal) sent him into severe depression. His problems were aggravated by the medical intervention, which was designed to stop the highs.

The 'lows' are treated with antidepressants while the highs are managed by mood stabilisers. So keeping Andrew flat is considered successful treatment. It sure doesn't feel successful to Andrew. Getting the right dose of the right medication is somewhat theoretical. For many people like Andrew, the medication keeps them emotionally very flat. They also have to live with the side-effects.

Naively, I asked Andrew, "Why don't you adjust the mood stabiliser to just stay a little high?" to which he replied, "It's like being an aeroplane on the runway, you can't stay there; you've got to take off."

The role of a counsellor in the lives of people such as Andrew is worth looking at. To do that, I'd like to clarify how I view counselling, and its role in the broader field of what could be called a severe emotional and mental disorder. People who have a crisis that remains overwhelming, benefit from having a safe place where they can off-load. This could take the form of a real friend; one who listens and goes on listening and treats all that is said with total confidentiality.

The maturity of a friend is revealed when the need of the wounded warrior exceeds the friend's expertise and they are able to say, "You need someone who has more skills than I have, and just as importantly, someone who isn't involved."

Ideally, that next level of support is a counsellor.

Co-dependence

I am using the word co-dependence as a term that we've become familiar with. I need to describe in some detail how I see this behaviour. First, I believe that we are all co-dependent to some degree; some more than others. It is a need to keep someone else happy or to be kept happy by someone or something else. For example, for a long time I thought I was the giver of happiness; but over time I realised that I was both the giver and the receiver.

This revelation was made clear to me by a young man who was trying desperately to be real with himself. He recounted that while visiting his parents, he realised he let his mother take care of him and when he was with his father, he changed roles, and sought to keep his father happy.

So we all start off in co-dependent relationships. As a baby, we are cared for mainly by our mother and rely on her to keep us happy. How often we enjoy doing something to make our child or grandchild happy; doing all we can to stop them crying, being upset or unhappy.

With that kind of initiation we are caught up with the expectation that others will make us happy or we need to keep others happy. We learn that being nice and cooperative often gets us what we want.

Failure at this game results in tantrums; the acting out feelings of anger, rejection, and not feeling loved.

We learn the role of parenting from our own parents. If we felt unloved, it is not too difficult to realise that, as parents, some of us are committed to loving our children as we weren't loved. This usually means overprotecting them; keeping them pain free. Giving them choices doesn't even get on the radar. If we haven't resolved these parent/child relationships ourselves, we react in response to what was done to us. Therefore, we are still controlled by our parents.

It is perhaps timely to put an individual's internal

painful journey into the context of their wider, external world.

The majority of people I saw were women of all ages, most of whom attended because they had run out of gas fulfilling the role of propping up family members, especially husbands. Encouraging them to be real and escape their co-dependent relationships required me to give them a very sobering warning.

If you decide to go down this very difficult path, there are some realities you need to be aware of:

- ❖ The co-dependent relationship is over. It's dead in the water. Keeping others happy is no longer an option. It doesn't mean that everything is over; just your part in the co-dependence.

- ❖ You are the only one who is trying to be different. The rest of the family and friends still expect you to be manipulated into doing what they want of you. Their comments of your new way of dealing with issues concerning them imply that you are being very selfish. It's about putting your inner, precious child into the group of people who you care about.

- ❖ You are going to lose a number of people from your life who you thought would be there for you. In contrast, there will be one or two people who will turn up, who you would never have expected.

❖ It can be extremely lonely, and isolating. Very few people go down, and stay on, this painfully precious road.

This process is never-ending. The character building occurs by continuing to go down this path, in a world that continues to present the co-dependent games as being real. The subtlety of the world's way is that it says that instantaneous pleasures will give us lasting happiness. In this world there is no such thing. It takes a long time to discover this deception. The best that we can acquire is an inner peace in the midst of the current crisis we are working through.

The antithesis of co-dependence is being emotionally real; first with God and ourselves, and then with significant others.

One of my profound sadnesses in supporting the terminally ill was observing that many of them regretted how they had wasted their lives pursuing goals that in their current reality seemed such a waste. At a minute to midnight, they were trying to live—truly live—before they died.

Dr Steele Fitchett, *Being Real: The Narrow Way to Loving Ourselves.*

Bipolar—Linda Ruth Brooks

Bipolar Disorder was previously known as Manic Depression. Its defining feature is the recurrent cycling from a state of euphoric elation to a state of depression. The severity of these extremes varies with each individual sufferer. It is important to remember that bipolar is a physiological brain function condition and the actions of the person during the extremes may not represent the values and personality of the sufferer. Bipolar often exhibits itself in the late teen years and early twenties. There is some evidence to suggest a genetic link.

In the manic state the condition is distinguished by a disconnection with reality and is differentiated from a normal sense of wellbeing and joy by the sense the person feels untouchable or invincible. Feelings of sadness, awareness of others are often numbed in this phase. The mania may reach peaks where rational thought is lost. It is quite common for this feeling of invincibility to be accompanied by acts of recklessness. The person may become disinhibited. They may become involved in activities that they wouldn't normally undertake, speeding, excessive drug and alcohol consumption or wanton sexual exploits. The disconnection with reality during this period results in the sufferer possessing a diminished ability to reason from cause to effect. There is a lack of awareness of natural consequences.

In the period before slipping into the irrational sphere, the person may be very productive, perform creatively at a high level and glow with optimism. Many sufferers describe mania 'being on top of the world' 'better than any drug' 'fully alive to themselves and the world'. There is a sense of being able to achieve anything. They appear unstoppable, a force of nature.

Many sufferers court the manic state, desperate to recreate the euphoria and elation that would quickly wear thin with non-sufferers. It is very difficult for non-sufferers to comprehend the allure of the manic phase when it is inevitably followed by the depths of depression.

The person has an increase in confidence, an inflated sense of self and an unrealistic concept of their abilities. This is often accompanied by irritability and distractibility.

The manic person may require very little sleep, have a change in appetite, their speech may be fast and erratic. If they slide into irrational thought and actions it becomes obvious to everyone but the sufferer that a brick wall is inevitable. It is very difficult for family and friends. At this stage the manic person has become a train wreck waiting to happen. They will take on unnecessary tasks, or repeat the same behaviour. Aggressive, loud and abusive language may be used on strangers and friends.

When disinhibited, they may strip naked at

inappropriate times and place, chase vehicles in road rage episodes. They may have a 'God-like' delusion that they have a quest to carry out, and react vigorously when opposed. In their own minds these actions seem perfectly acceptable.

Because sufferers experience the manic state as beneficial and comfortable, they often present initially for medical assistance in the depressive phase and are unable, or unaware, of the nature and presence of mania.

The depressive phase of the condition may best be described as 'free fall' to the depths of despair. The sufferer may be able to articulate a trigger, but often the gloom is unexpected and all encompassing. When depressed, many sufferers state that all feeling is absent. There is lethargy, increased fatigue, feelings of worthlessness and often anxiety. These many be accompanied by a profound sense of shame for any irrational acts that occurred during the manic phase. Suicide ideation may be present.

Professional assistance and support is beneficial. An awareness of the condition and its presentation, symptoms and impact is an essential starting point. Once diagnosed, the process of treatment is individualised. Medication is often a part of treatment, but a significant number of bipolar sufferers are able to maintain a satisfactory life by managing their symptoms by other methods such as counselling and self-regulation. The cultivation of nurturing and supportive relationships are key factors to management, along with the development of strategies to lessen the extremes of the condition.

As a registered nurse who has cared for many people with bipolar, and been blessed by association with sufferers I feel it is important to realise that bipolar is separate from personality and character traits. Like the rest of humanity there are people who are kind, generous, courageous and devoted to others. Their behaviour in the manic or depressive phase bears little resemblance to their morality and integrity. Some sufferers have a different way of viewing people and moving in the world that is driven by factors other than bipolar. It would be a travesty for all bipolar sufferers to be branded by the selfish, criminal or antisocial actions of this group by attaching these behaviours to the condition of bipolar.

Useful references

SFNSW

www.sfnsw.org.au/questions/discussion.htm

Mental Illness Fellowship Australia

www.mifa.org.au

Mental Illness Fellowship Victoria

www.mifellowship.org

Mental Health Services Website (Vic)

www.health.vic.gov.au/mentalhealth

National Alliance of the Mentally Ill

(NAMI) (USA)

www.nami.org

Mental Health Council of Australia

www.mhca.com.au

SANE Australia

www.sane.org

Beyond Blue

www.beyondblue.org.au

Author

Linda Brooks lives in Paradise, also known as the east coast of Australia. She has two sons who think their only job in life is to keep both her feet on the ground. She is addicted to sunshine, large bodies of water and living life to the full. She gained the attention of a publisher when her short stories found critical acclaim on the ABC website, 'The Making of Modern Australia' and her first published book resulted, *A Curious & Inelegant Childhood*, a memoir of growing up in rural Australia. Brooks explores the gamut of human experience with fearless clarity and buoyant optimism. Her trademark wit and sharp observation is crafted with depth and compassion.

Linda has written and illustrated children's' books, fiction and poetry. Linda's short stories have been published in numerous anthologies: Coastlines 5 & 6 (Southern Cross University), Wood, Bricks & Stone (Catchfire Press) and Grieve (Hunter Writer's Centre) and Longing for Solitude (Stringybark Press). She has won creative writing awards, including first prize for The Legacy University Level Creative Writing Award and first prize for the Gabe Reynaud Creative Writing Award, and the Mater Misericordiae Grieve Writing Award. Linda's books feature her skill as an artist and illustrator.

Other titles by Linda

Nonfiction:
A Curious & Inelegant Childhood
'I'm not broken, I'm just different'
(on Asperger's with Professor Tony Attwood)

Adult fiction:
Behind Whispering Hands
The Unprize
Scarlett doesn't live here anymore
A broken hallelujah
Under the Bracken Fern

Children's books:
A Tabby Never Forgets
An Angels Tears
Beth's Christmas Wish
Callan the Chameleon
(on Asperger's with Professor Tony Attwood)
Dusty Bunny's Very Important Job
Ethereal Land
Izzy & Pudding the Cat
I want a monkey!
Madam Iris Bigglesworth
The Banyula Series (with teacher's prompts)
The Frog that Hiccupped
When the stars move
Who Stole Christmas?

Publisher of the anthologies:
'We are Australian'
The Great Australian Shed
Waltzing Matilda

www.ingramcontent.com/pod-product-compliance
Lightning Source LLC
Chambersburg PA
CBHW011614290426
44110CB00020BA/2585